Rhode Island Lighthouses

A Pictorial History

Rhode Island Lighthouses

A Pictorial History

Richard Holmes

Rhode Island Lighthouses: A Pictorial History

By Richard Holmes

Rhodeislandlighthousehistory.info Publishing
PO Box 6161
Fall River, MA 02724

Library of Congress Control Card Number: 2008941680

ISBN: 978-0-615-26322-9

10 9 8 7 6 5 4 3 2

Printed the United States

This book is dedicated to my family and the lighthouse keepers
who served at Rhode Island Lighthouses.

Acknowledgements

I would like to thank the US Coast Guard Historian's Office for their help in researching this book. I would also like to thank the National Archives and Records Administration's Still Picture Branch for their help in locating some the photographs in this book.

I would like to take Wayne Wheeler of the United States Lighthouse Society for his him in reseaching this book.

Entered according to Act of Congress, in the year of our Lord 1869, by
Manchester Brothers, in the Clerk's Office of the District Court
of the District of Rhode Island.

IDA LEWIS,

In Costume as in the Rescue of March 29th, 1869.

Contents

Beavertail Lighthouse 1

Block Island North Lighthouse 8

Block Island Southeast Lighthouse 11

Brenton Reef Lights 16

Brenton Reef Lightship: LV-14 17

Brenton Reef Lightship: LV-11 18

Brenton Reef Lightship: LV-39 22

Brenton Reef Lightship: LV-102/WAL 525 26

Brenton Reef Offshore Light station 31

Narragansett Bay Entrance Lighted Horn Buoy NB 34

Bristol Ferry Lighthouse 37

Bullock Point Lighthouse 45

Castle Hill Lighthouse 52

Conanicut Island Lighthouse 56

Conimicut Shoal Lighthouse 63

Dutch Island Lighthouse 68

Fuller Rock Lighthouse 73

Gould Island Lighthouse 75

Gull Rocks Lighthouse 78

Hog Island Shoal Lights 86

Hog Island Shoal Lightship: LV-12 87

Hog Island Shoal Lighthouse 90

Lime Rock Lighthouse 95

Mussel Bed Shoals Lighthouse 110

Nayatt Point Lighthouse 116

Newport Harbor Lighthouse 123

Plum Beach Lighthouse 131

Point Judith Lighthouse 139

Pomham Rocks Lighthouse 153

Poplar Point Lighthouse 156

Prudence Island Lighthouse 161

Rose Island Lighthouse 164

Sabin Point Lighthouse 166

Sakonnet Point Lighthouse 171

Sassafras Point Lighthouse 178

Warwick Lighthouse 180

Watch Hill Lighthouse 184

Whale Rock Lighthouse 193

Wickford Harbor Lighthouse 198

Glossary 203

Bibliography 206

Index 210

Beavertail Lighthouse

Location: Beavertail Point on the southern tip of Conanicut Island

Established: 1749

Current Lighthouse Constructed: 1856

Automated: 1972

Original Illuminating Apparatus: Third-order Fresnel lens

Current Illuminating Apparatus: DCB 24

Height: 45 feet

Status: Active aid to navigation - Museum in assistant keeper's dwelling

Light Characteristic: Flashing White every 6 seconds

Range: 15 miles

Courtesy of N.L. Stebbins

Beavertail Lighthouse in 1898.

Beavertail Lighthouse in the 1890's.

Beavertail Lighthouse in the early twentieth century.

The 1856 Beavertail Lighthouse's keeper's dwelling and granite light tower.

Beavertail Lighthouse in the 1920s. In 1898, a brick addition, an assistant keeper's dwelling, was built on the left side of the 1856 Beavertail Lighthouse keeper's dwelling and granite light tower.

The fog signal building at Beavertail Lighthouse in the 1890s. It was equipped with two ten inch steam whistles.

The fog signal building at Beavertail Lighthouse in the early twentieth century. In 1900, the fog signal was changed from two ten inch steam whistles to two second class automatic sirens.

The lantern at Beavertail Lighthouse. In 1991 the fourth order Fresnel lens was removed from the lantern. It was replaced with a DCB-24 search light.

The foundation of the 1754 Beavertail Light tower.

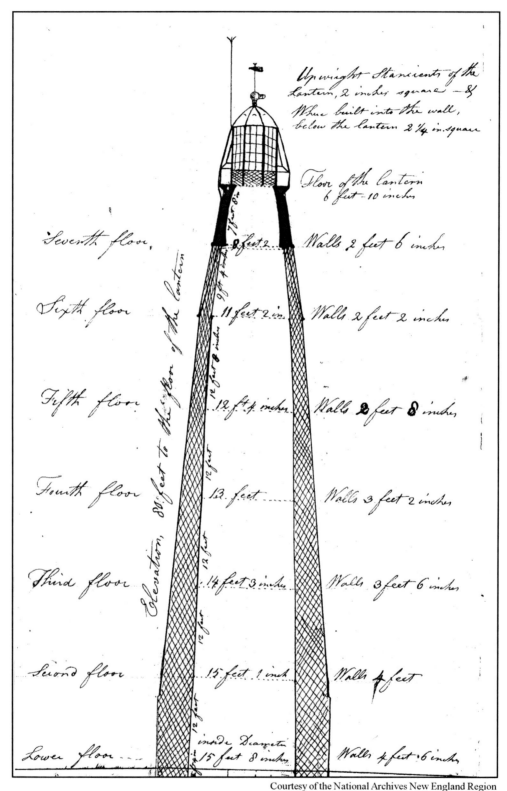

A cross section of the 1754 Beavertail Lighthouse.

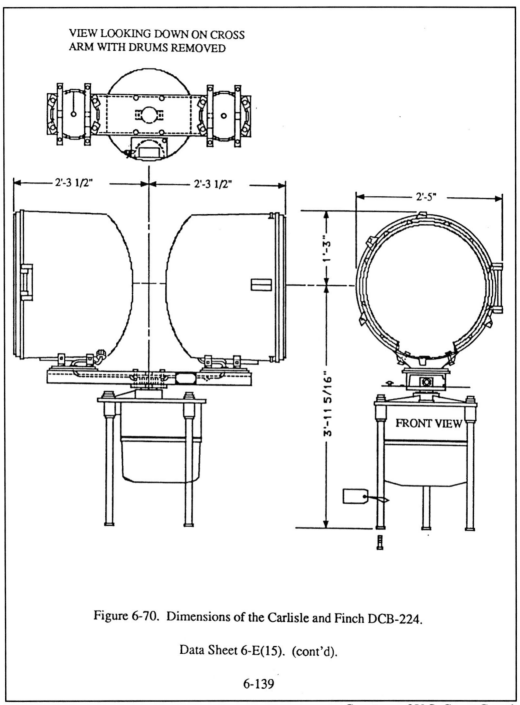

VIEW LOOKING DOWN ON CROSS
ARM WITH DRUMS REMOVED

2'-3 1/2"   2'-3 1/2"   2'-5"

1'-3"

3'-11 5/16"

FRONT VIEW

Figure 6-70. Dimensions of the Carlisle and Finch DCB-224.

Data Sheet 6-E(15). (cont'd).

6-139

Courtesy of U.S. Coast Guard

The Carisle and Finch DCB-24 is the light now installed at Beavertail. The DCB-24 and
DCB-224 are the Coast Guard's standard rotating searchlights. They are used at
lighthouses that must have a range greater than 18 miles.

Block Island North Lighthouse

Location: Northern tip of Block Island

Established: 1829

Current Lighthouse Constructed: 1867

Automated: 1955

Deactivated: 1973 -1989

Original Illuminating Apparatus: Fourth-order Fresnel lens

Current Illuminating Apparatus: VBR 25

Height: 55 feet

Status: Active aid to navigation - Museum

Light Characteristic: Flashing White every 5 seconds

Range: 13 miles

NORTH LIGHT HOUSE, BLOCK ISLAND, R.I.

This is the fourth Block Island North Lighthouse. Its first keeper was Hiram Bell. He served at the lighthouse until 1891.

Courtesy National Archives, photo no. 26-LG-11-14

This was the fourth lighthouse built on the northern tip of Block Island. It was built in 1867 to replace the 1857 Block Island North Lighthouse because erosion was undermining its foundation. The older lighthouse was torn down and was used to protect the area around the new lighthouse from the destructive action of the wind.

Courtesy National Archives, photo no. 26-LG-11-14

Block Island Island North Lighthouse's lantern and fourth order Fresnel lens.

Courtesy National Archives, photo no. 26-LG-11-14

The front entrance to Block Island North Lighthouse.

Block Island Southeast Lighthouse

Location: Mohegan Bluffs on Block Island's southern coast

Established: 1875

Lighthouse Constructed: 1874

Deactivated: 1990 - 1994

Original Illuminating Apparatus: First-order Fresnel lens

Current Illuminating Apparatus: First-order Fresnel lens

Height: 67 feet

Status: Active aid to navigation - Museum

Light Characteristic: Flashing Green every 5 seconds

Range: 20 miles

SOUTH EAST LIGHTHOUSE. BLOCK ISLAND, R. I.

Block Island Southeast Lighthouse was built in 1874 by contractor T.H. Tynan.

Block Island Southeast Lighthouse's cast iron lantern was made by Paulding, Kemble & Company.

SOUTH LIGHT & FOG HORNS, BLOCK ISLAND, R. I.

Block Island Southeast Lighthouse and its second fog signal building.

In 1929, Block Island Southeast Lighthouse's first Fresnel lens was moved to another lighthouse. A new first order lens, consisting of just eight lens panels, was placed in the lighthouse. It was replaced with another first order Fresnel lens in 1994, when the lighthouse was relighted.

The South Light, Block Island, R. I.

Block Island Southeast Lighthouse's first fog signal, a steam powered siren, located in the shed in the middle of this postcard, was built in 1873. It was destroyed by fire in 1906. The fog signal was moved to the dark colored building just to the right of the lighthouse.

A compressed air fog signal with kerosene engines was installed in this building in 1908, after Block Island Southeast Lighthouse's first fog signal building burned down. The Coast Guard tore this building down in 1987.

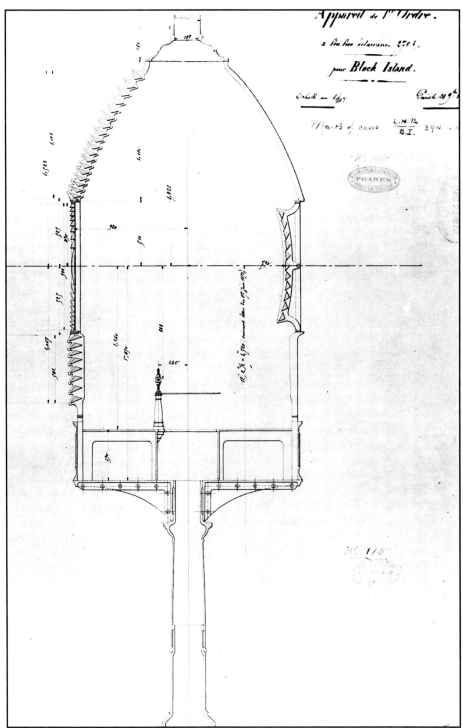

This is a diagram of Block Island Southeast Lighthouse's original first order Fresnel lens. It was built by Barbier and Fenestre in 1873. It was used at Block Island Lighthouse from 1874 to 1929.

Brenton Reef Lights

Brenton Beef Lightship: LV-14
1853 - 1856

Brenton Reef Lightship: LV-11
1856 - 1897

Brenton Reef Lightship: LV-39
1897 - 1935

Brenton Reef Lightship: LV-102/WAL-525
1935 - 1962

Brenton Reef Offshore Light station
1962 - 1992

Narragansett Bay Entrance Lighted Horn Buoy NB
1992 - present

Brenton Reef Lightship : LV-14

Location: Entrance to East Passage of Narragansett Bay

Year Built: 1852

Design: Wood - white oak and yellow pine; copper and iron fastened; 2 masts (foremast higher) daymarks on both

Length: 91' (lbp) **Beam:** 22' **Draft:** 9' **Tonnage:** 159 gross

Illuminating Apparatus: Single lantern with 8 lard oil lamps

Propulsion: Sail - sloop rigged

Years on Station: 1853 - 1856

Status: Sold at auction in 1872

Light Characteristic: Fixed White

Range: 12.5 miles

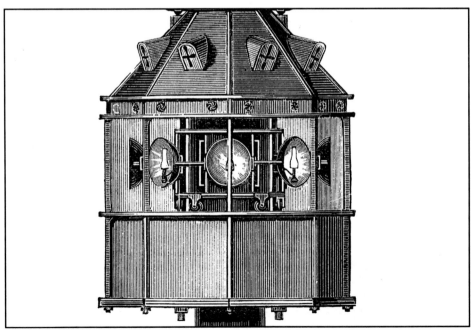

These were the types of lanterns and lamps that were used on lightships like Brenton Reef Lightship LV-14.

Brenton Reef Lightship: LV-11

Location: Entrance to East Passage of Narragansett Bay

Year Built: 1853

Design: Wood - white oak; copper and iron fastened; 2 masts with daymarks on both mastheads

Length: 104' (lbp) **Beam:** 24' 8" **Draft:** 9' 10" **Tonnage:** 320 gross

Illuminating Apparatus: 2 lanterns, each having 8 constant level oil lamps

Propulsion: Sail - schooner rig; fore and main carried on Spencer masts

Years on Station: 1856 - 1897

Status: Sold 1927

Light Characteristic: Fixed White

Range: 12 miles

Courtesy National Archives, photo no. 26-LG-11-1

Brenton Reef Lightship LV-11's hand operated 1050 pound fogbell.

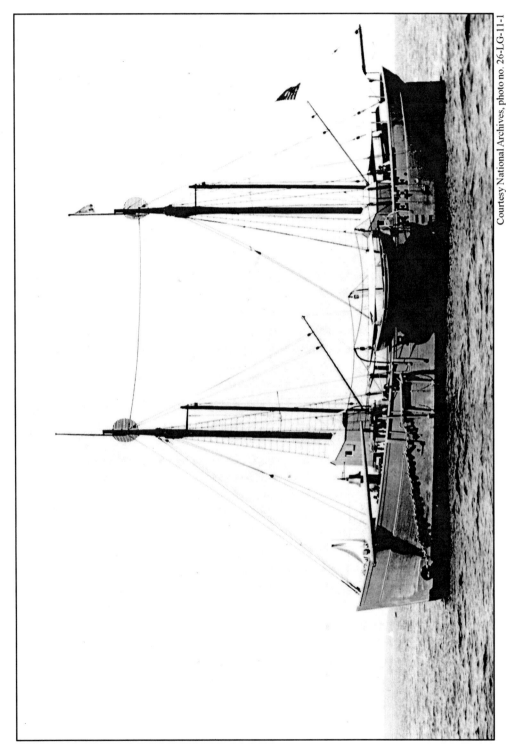

Courtesy National Archives, photo no. 26-LG-11-1

Brenton Reef Lightship LV-11 was damaged in 1890, when the British streamer Curlew ran into it. The lightship was taken off station and was repaired. It was put back on station on July 22, 1891.

Courtesy National Archives, photo no. 26-LG-11-1

This small building on Brenton Reef Lightship LV-11 was used to store the lantern during the day. At night the roof would be opened and the lantern would be pulled to the top of the mast.

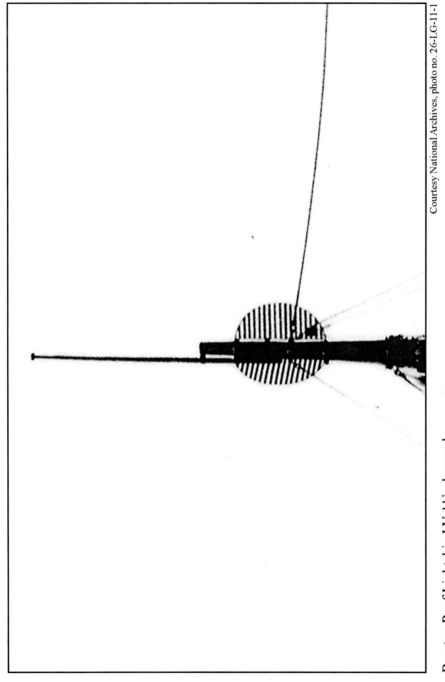

Brenton Reef Lightship LV-11's daymark.

Brenton Reef Lightship: LV-39

Location: Entrance to East Passage of Narragansett Bay

Year Built: 1875

Design: Wood - white oak and locust; copper and galvanized iron fastened; 2 masts, daymarks on both; smokestack forward of mainmast; 2 auxiliary steam boilers, steam pump and steam fog signal machinery

Length: 119' 6" (lbp) **Beam:** 22' 9" **Draft:** 12' 6" **Tonnage:** 387 gross

Illuminating Apparatus: 2 lanterns, each with 8 Argand fountain burner oil lamps

Propulsion: Sail-sloop rig; fore and main carried on Spencer masts

Years on Station: 1897 - 1935

Status: Sank in 1975 while being towed to a shipyard in Beverly, Massachusetts.

Light Characteristic: 1887 - 1921 Fixed White; 1921 - 1935 Occulting White every 4 seconds

Range: 1897 - 1921 11.5 miles; 1921 -1935 12 miles

Brenton Reef Lightship LV-39's fogbell.

Brenton Reef Lightship LV-39 right side.

Brenton Reef Lightship LV-39's left side.

Courtesy National Archives, photo no. 26-G-126-21132

Brenton Reef Lightship LV-39's commanding officer.

Brenton Reef Lightship LV-39's crewmen.

Brenton Reef Lightship: LV-102/WAL 525

Location: Entrance to East Passage of Narragansett Bay

Year Built: 1916

Design: Self propelled; steel whaleback hull; single large diameter tubular lantern mast forward; steel pilot house/bridge at foot of mast; small jigger mast aft

Length: 119' 10" (loa) **Beam:** 25' **Draft:** 11' 4" **Tonnage:** 360 displacement

Illuminating Apparatus: 1935 - 1955 Fifth-order Fresnel lens mounted in large cylindrical lantern; 1955 - 1962 Duplex 375 mm lens lantern

Propulsion: One 200 HP Mietz and Weiss 4 cylinder 2 cycle direct reversing kerosene engine driving 4 bladed propeller; speed 8 knots

Years on Station: 1935 - 1962

Status: Decommissioned at Boston October 25, 1963.

Light Characteristic: Occulting White every 4 seconds

Range: 13 miles 1935 - 1946; 12 miles 1946 - 1962

Courtesy of Coast Guard Historisn's Office

Brenton Reef Lightship LV-102/WAL-525's pilot house.

Brenton Reef Lightship LV-102/WAL 525 was placed on Brenton Reef on March 27, 1935.

Courtesy of Coast Guard Historisn's Office

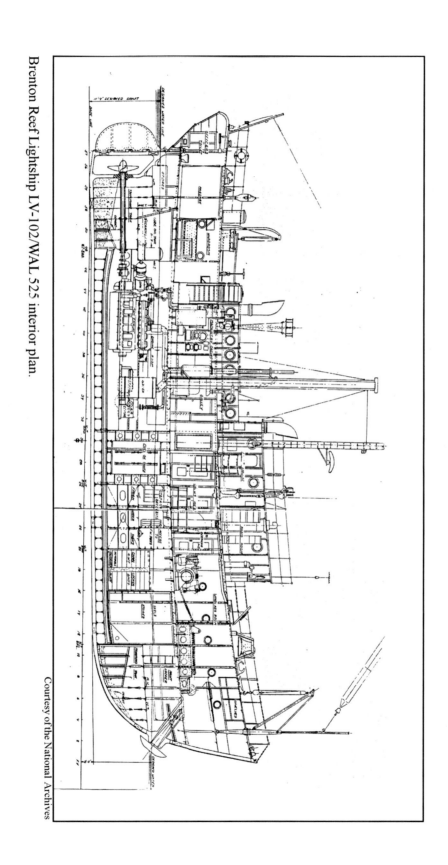

Brenton Reef Lightship LV-102/WAL 525 interior plan.

Courtesy of the National Archives

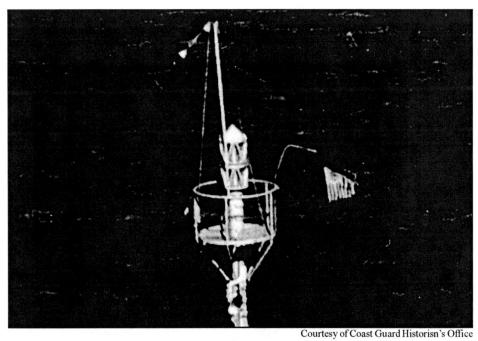

This Duplex 375 mm lens lantern was installed on the Brenton Reef Lightship LV-102/WAL 525 in 1955.

Brenton Reef Lightship LV-102/WAL 525's hand operated 700-lb bell.

Brenton Reef Lightship LV-102/WAL 525's fog signal.

Brenton Reef Offshore Light station

Location: Entrance to West Passage of Narragansett Bay

Year Built: 1962

Design: A deckhouse supported by four cross-braced steel legs extending 25 feet into bedrock beneath the ocean floor.

Illuminating Apparatus: Crouse Hinds, Double Drum Double Ended DCE-36 Airways Beacon

Height 87 feet

Years on Station 1962 - 1992

Status: Dismantled in 1992

Light Characteristic: Two Group flashing white every 10 seconds

Range: 15 miles

Courtesy of Coast Guard Historisn's Office

Brenton Reef Offshore Light station's deckhouse. It was an unmanned light.

Courtesy of Coast Guard Historisn's Office

Brenton Reef Offshore Light station was built in 1962 to replace Brenton Reef Lightship LV-102/WAL 525. It was removed in 1992 because it had become too expensive to maintain and service. It was replaced by a 9X35 LWR buoy.

Courtesy of Coast Guard Historisn's Office

Brenton Reef Offshore Light station's main optic, the spotlight shaped object on the left side of the photograph, was a Crouse Hinds, double-drum double-ended DCB-36 Airways Beacon equipped with 1000 watt lamps.

Narragansett Bay Entrance Lighted Horn Buoy NB

Location: Entrance to East Passage of Narragansett Bay

Year Placed on Station: 1992

Design: The buoy consists of a counterweight, the buoy hull, and a tower.

Height 36' 5 ½"

Weight 18,500 lbs.

Illuminating Apparatus: 155 mm lens

Status: Active aid to navigation

Light Characteristic: Flashing White every 4 seconds

Range: 9 miles.

A 9X35 LWR buoy on a Coast Guard buoy tender. This is not the Narragansett Bay Entrance Lighted Horn Buoy NB. It's a similar 9X35LWR bouy off Honolulu Harbor.

2.K. 1.   <u>9X35LWR</u>. The 9X35LWR is designed and constructed for the most exposed
locations. It has an open counterweight tube to accomodate a whistle,
horn, or wave turbine generator (WTG). The tower can accomodate a racon,
flashtube, and passing light. Mounting holes are provided at the base of the
tower for solar panels.

a.   <u>Standard Buoy Arrangements.</u> 1987 Type 9X35LWR, 9X35LR,
9X35LHR.

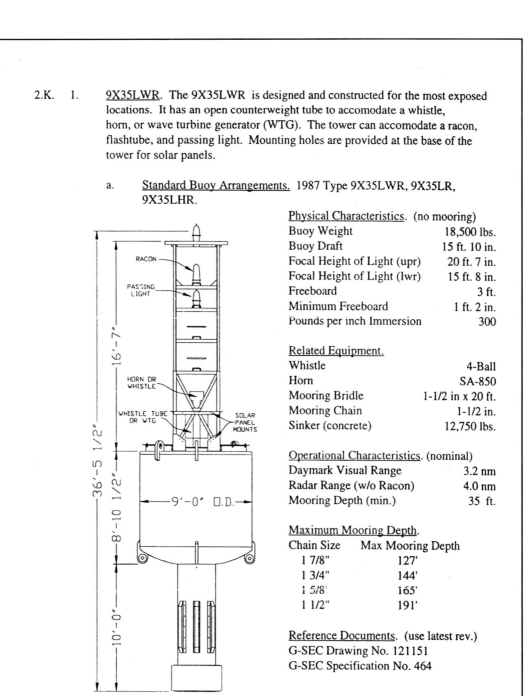

<u>Physical Characteristics.</u> (no mooring)
Buoy Weight	18,500 lbs.
Buoy Draft	15 ft. 10 in.
Focal Height of Light (upr)	20 ft. 7 in.
Focal Height of Light (lwr)	15 ft. 8 in.
Freeboard	3 ft.
Minimum Freeboard	1 ft. 2 in.
Pounds per inch Immersion	300

<u>Related Equipment.</u>
Whistle	4-Ball
Horn	SA-850
Mooring Bridle	1-1/2 in x 20 ft.
Mooring Chain	1-1/2 in.
Sinker (concrete)	12,750 lbs.

<u>Operational Characteristics.</u> (nominal)
Daymark Visual Range	3.2 nm
Radar Range (w/o Racon)	4.0 nm
Mooring Depth (min.)	35 ft.

<u>Maximum Mooring Depth.</u>
Chain Size	Max Mooring Depth
1 7/8"	127'
1 3/4"	144'
1 5/8'	165'
1 1/2"	191'

<u>Reference Documents.</u> (use latest rev.)
G-SEC Drawing No. 121151
G-SEC Specification No. 464

Data Sheet 2.K.1. 9X35LWR buoy.

CH-3   2-42

The 9X35 LWR buoy replaced the Brenton Reef Offshore Light station in 1992. It was first
equipped with a whistle, but was later replaced by a horn.

Courtesy of U.S. Coast Guard Digital

A 9X35 LWR buoy at sea. This is not the Narragansett Bay Entrance Lighted Horn Buoy NB. It's a similar 9X35 LWR bouy off Honolulu Harbor.

Bristol Ferry Lighthouse

Location: Entrance to Mount Hope Bay

Established: 1855

Current Lighthouse Constructed: 1855

Deactivated: 1927

Original Illuminating Apparatus: Fourth-order Fresnel lens

Current Illuminating Apparatus: None

Height: 34 feet

Status: Private Residence

Light Characteristic: None

Range: None

Bristol Ferry Lighthouse was built in 1855 to replace a light maintained by The Old Colony Steamboat Company.

Bristol Ferry Lighthouse was first lighted on October 4, 1955.

Bristol Ferry Lighthouse was sold in 1929 for $2,050.

Courtesy of Coast Guard Historian's Office

Bristol Ferry Lighthouse and its keeper in 1884.

A Bristol Ferry lighthouse keeper in 1884. The keeper may be Edward P. Hoxsie.

Bristol Ferry Lighthouse's entrance.

Courtesy of Coast Guard Historian's Office

In 1916 the lighthouse's tower was extended by six feet to accommodate a new lantern.

Bristol Ferry Lighthouse's wooden lantern in 1884.

In 1916 an inspection found Bristol Ferry lighthouse's wooden lantern to be in very poor condition and it needed to be replaced. This iron lantern from the discontinued Rondout Lighthouse in New York was placed on the lighthouse in 1917. It was removed when the lighthouse was deactivated in 1927.

ADDRESS ALL COMMUNICATIONS TO
SUPERINTENDENT OF LIGHTHOUSES
STATEN ISLAND, N.Y.

WJL:FM

DEPARTMENT OF COMMERCE

LIGHTHOUSE SERVICE

28857 E

15 1929 APR 10 AM 8:56

Received

4/16/29 With Dept.

GENERAL DEPOT
OFFICE SUPERINTENDENT OF LIGHTHOUSES
3D DISTRICT, STATEN ISLAND, N.Y.

April 8, 1929.

Commissioner of Lighthouses.

SUBJECT: Sale of Portion of Bristol Ferry Light Station
Reservation.

REFERENCE: Form S-3, Survey of Public Property, dated
October 6, approved by Department without date,
and Bureau's approval of November 15, 1928.

1. Bids were opened at this office on April 4 for the
sale of a portion of Bristol Ferry Light Station Reservation.
The highest bid received was that of Anna Santulli in the
amount of $2050.00, which bid is recommended for acceptance.

2. Attached is an abstract of the bids received together
with the bids. Also attached is a statement of the parties
invited to bid, including statement where notices were posted.
Attached also is copy of the Form 128, Newspaper Advertisement.

3. Also forwarded herewith is deed in triplicate for
execution if the above recommendation is approved.

J. T. YATES,

KSG-FBW
2 Incls.

Bureau of Lighthouses, Washington, D. C.
May 6, 1929.

Returned to the Supt. of Lighthouses, Staten Island, N. Y. Accept-
ance of the bid of Anna Santulli in the amount of $2,050 for a portion of
the Bristol Ferry Light Station has been approved by the Department. The
deed conveying this property to the successful bidder has also been executed
by the Department and two copies thereof are returned herewith together with
all bids submitted with your above letter.

Acting Commissioner of Lighthouses.

An April 8, 1929 letter to the Commissioner of Lighthouses about the sale of the Bristol Ferry
Light Station.

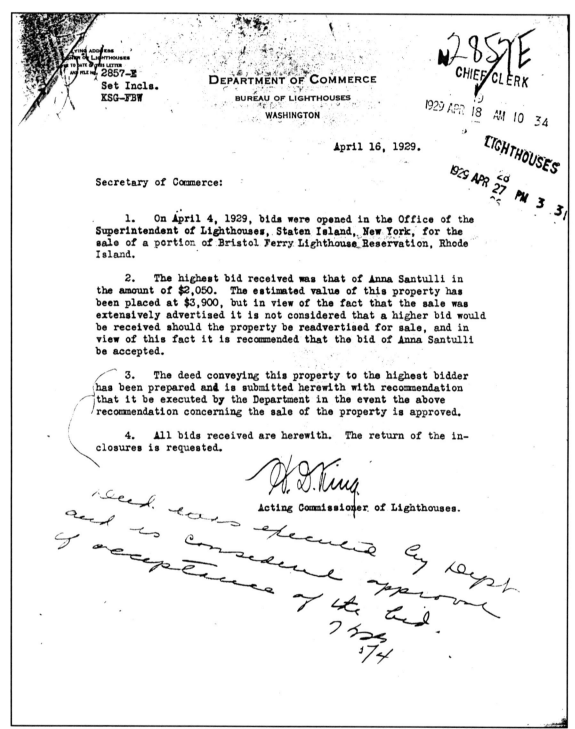

DEPARTMENT OF COMMERCE

BUREAU OF LIGHTHOUSES

WASHINGTON

2857-E
Set Incls.
KSG-FBW

April 16, 1929.

Secretary of Commerce:

1. On April 4, 1929, bids were opened in the Office of the Superintendent of Lighthouses, Staten Island, New York, for the sale of a portion of Bristol Ferry Lighthouse Reservation, Rhode Island.

2. The highest bid received was that of Anna Santulli in the amount of $2,050. The estimated value of this property has been placed at $3,900, but in view of the fact that the sale was extensively advertised it is not considered that a higher bid would be received should the property be readvertised for sale, and in view of this fact it is recommended that the bid of Anna Santulli be accepted.

3. The deed conveying this property to the highest bidder has been prepared and is submitted herewith with recommendation that it be executed by the Department in the event the above recommendation concerning the sale of the property is approved.

4. All bids received are herewith. The return of the inclosures is requested.

H. D. King

Acting Commissioner of Lighthouses.

Courtesy of the National Archives

An April 16, 1929 letter to the Secretary of Commerce about the sale of the Bristol Ferry Light Station.

Bullock's Point Lighthouse

Location: Providence River near Bullock's Point

Established: 1872

Lighthouse Constructed: 1876

Removed: 1939

Original Illuminating Apparatus: Six-order Fresnel lens

Current Illuminating Apparatus: 250 mm lens

Height: 35 feet

Status: Active aid to navigation - Skeleton tower

Light Characteristic: Occulting White every 4 seconds

Range: 4 miles

A portable beacon was built at Bullock's Point in 1872. A keeper would row out to it at sunset to light the beacon and row back out to it in the morning to extinguish it. The portable beacon was replaced with a lighthouse in 1876.

Riprap boat leeway too cramped for rough weather landing.

Canopy to be removed

Deck to be replaced

Rebuild riprap

Bullock;s Point Lighthouse's first keeper was appointed on November 7, 1872. His annual salary was $500.00.

Courtesy of Coast Guard Historian's Office

Courtesy of Coast Guard Historian's Office

A Bullock's Point Lighthouse keeper, possibly John J. Card.

Bulllock's Point Lighthouse's lantern and sixth order Fresnel lens.

Courtesy of Coast Guard Historian's Office

Bullock's Point Lighthouse after the 1938 Hurricane.

Bullock's Point Lighthouse's last keeper, Andrew Zuius, was trapped at the lighthouse during the 1938 Hurricane. Wind driven waves tore the walls off of the lighthouse. Water poured into the lighthouse, washing the furniture out. Zuius had to go to the lighthouse's second floor so he wouldn't be washed out of it. Just minutes after he climbed the stairs to the second floor, a huge wave tore them away. Andrew kept the light burning through the night.

Bullock's Point Lighthouse was torn down in 1939. It was replaced with a skeleton tower.

Bullock's Point Lighthouse's base and skeleton tower.

Castle Hill Lighthouse

Location: Castle Hill

Established: 1890

Lighthouse Constructed: 1890

Automated: 1957

Original Illuminating Apparatus: Fifth-order Fresnel lens

Current Illuminating Apparatus: 300 mm Lens

Height: 34 feet

Status: Active aid to navigation

Light Characteristic: Isophase Red every 6 seconds

Range: 12 miles

Alexander Agassig sold the government the land for Castle Hill Lighthouse on June 10, 1887 for $1.00.

Castle Hill Lighthouse in the early twentieth century. It was equipped with a fifth order Fresnel lens. A 2400-pound fogbell was installed at the lighthouse in 1897.

Castle Hill Lighthouse in 1999. The fifth order Fresnel lens was removed in 1957. It was replaced with a 300 mm plastic lens.

In November 1891, Castle Hill Lighthouse's first fog bell was removed. A 1298-pound fog bell was reinstalled in 1896. It was replaced with a 2400-pound fog bell in 1897.

The pipe shaped object on the front of the lantern is a FA-232 fog signal. It has a half-mile range.

Conanicut Island Lighthouse

Location: North end of Conanicut Island

Established: 1886

Lighthouse Constructed: 1886

Discontinued: 1930

Original Illuminating Apparatus: Fifth-order Fresnel lens

Current Illuminating Apparatus: None

Height: 50 feet

Status: Private Residence

Light Characteristic: None

Range: None

Courtesy National Archives, photo no. 26-LG-11-71

The lantern on Conanicut Lighthouse.

Courtesy National Archives, photo no. 26-LG-11-71

Conanicut Lighthouse was first lighthed on April 1, 1886. Horace Arnold was the first keeper.

Conanicut Island Lighthouse was closed in 1933. The fifth order Frensel lens and lantern were removed after it was closed. The lighthouse was sold at auction in 1934 for $2,874.

Courtesy National Archives, photo no. 26-LG-11-71

The building on the left is a fog signal building. The building on the right is an engine building.

Courtesy National Archives, photo no. 26-LG-11-71

Courtesy of Coast Guard Historisn's Office

A forty foot skeleton tower replaced Conanicut Lighthouse in 1933. It remained in service until the 1980s.

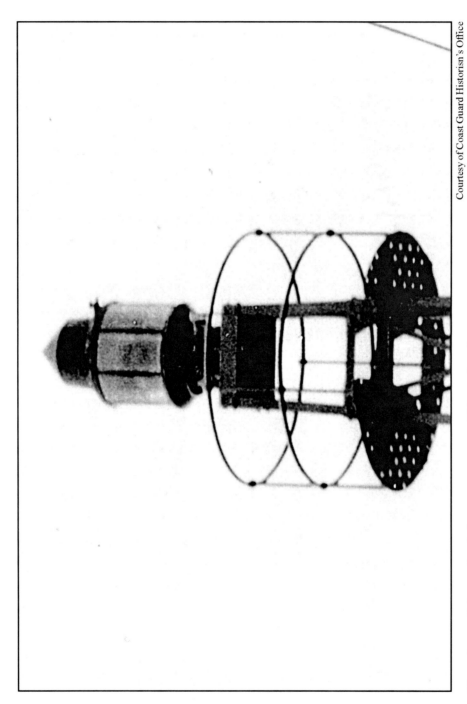

The primary light on the skeleton tower was a 375 mm lens lantern.

The skeleton tower had a 300 mm secondary lens lantern.

Conimicut Shoal Lighthouse

Location: Entrance to Providence River

Established: 1868

Original Lighthouse Constructed: 1868

Current Lighthouse Constructed: 1883

Automated: 1966

Original Illuminating Apparatus: Fourth-order Fresnel lens

Current Illuminating Apparatus: 250 mm lens

Height: 58 feet

Status: Active aid to navigation - Owned by city of Warwick, Rhode Island

Light Characteristic: Flashing White every 2.5 seconds

Range: 15 miles

Courtesy of N.L. Stebbins

In 1868, a granite daymark off Conimicut Point was converted to a lighthouse. It was replaced with the current lighthouse in 1883.

In 1960, Conimicut Lighthouse was the last lighthouse in America to be converted to electricity.

Conimicut Lighthouse in 1997.

Conimicut Lighthouse's lantern and watch room. A fourth order Frensel lens can be seen in the lantern. The lighthouse's fog signal, a fog bell, is located on the watch room gallery.

Conimicut Lighthouse's lantern and watch room in 1998. A 250 mm lens can be seen in the lantern. It replaced the lighthouse's fourth order Fresnel lens. A F-232 fog signal has replaced the fog bell.

Conimicut Lighthouse's first floor gallery in the early twentieth century.

Conimicut Lighthouse's first floor gallery in the 1960s.

Dutch Island Lighthouse

Location: Dutch Island

Established: 1826

Current Lighthouse Constructed: 1857

Deactivated: 1979–2007

Original Illuminating Apparatus: Fourth-order Fresnel lens

Current Illuminating Apparatus: Solar Powered Beacon

Height: 42 feet

Status: Private aid to navigation

Light Characteristic: Flashing Red every 6 seconds

Range: 3 miles

Courtesy of Coast Guard Historian's Office

Dutch Island Lighthouse and keeper.

The lantern at Dutch Island Lighthouse.

Dutch Island Lighthouse's fog bell. It was installed in 1878

A lighthouse keeper at Dutch Island Lighthouse.

A northern view of Dutch Island Lighthouse.

Dutch Island Light, Narragansett Bay, R. I.

Dutch Island Lighthouse was automated in 1947 and the fourth order Fresnel lens was replaced with a 375 mm lens.

A postcard of Dutch Island Lighthouse.

The unrestored Dutch Island Lighthouse in 2001. In 2007 after years of fundrasing by the Dutch Island Lighthouse Society, the lighthouse was restored. It was relighted on November 17, 2007.

Fuller Rock Lighthouse

Location: East side of Providence River near Providence

Established: 1874

Lighthouse Constructed: 1874

Removed: 1924

Original Illuminating Apparatus: Six-order Fresnel lens

Current Illuminating Apparatus: 250 mm lens

Height: 14 feet

Status: Active aid to navigation - Skeleton tower now named Channel Light 42

Light Characteristic: Isophase every 4 seconds

Range: 4 miles

Fuller Rock Light, Providence River, R. I.

Fuller Rock Light in the early twentieth century.

In 1923 Fuller Rock Light exploded during refueling operations and was destoryed .
Several crewmen on the lighthouse tender Pansy anchored near the light were injured.

Fuller Rock Light's granite base.

Gould Island Lighthouse

Location: East side of Gould Island

Established: 1889

Lighthouse Constructed: 1889

Deactivated: 1947

Original Illuminating Apparatus: Fifth-order Fresnel lens

Current Illuminating Apparatus: None

Height: 30 feet

Status: Torn down in 1960

Light Characteristic: None

Range: None

Gould Island Lighthouse and keeper's house.

Gould Island Lighthouse was built in 1889 to replace a private beacon.

Courtesy of N.L. Stebbins

Courtesy of N.L. Stebbins

Gould Island Lighthouse was closed in 1947 and was replaced with a skeleton tower.

Gull Rocks Lighthouse

Location: Near east side of the Newport Bridge

Established: 1887

Lighthouse Constructed: 1887

Discontinued: 1969

Original Illuminating Apparatus: Two lens lanterns

Current Illuminating Apparatus: None

Height: 40 feet

Status: Burned down in 1961

Light Characteristic: None

Range: None

Small lights called lens lanterns were hung from the east and west gables of Gull Rocks
Lighthouse from 1900 to 1928.

Courtesy of Coast Guard Historian's Office

The Old Colony Steamboat Company maintained an aid to navigation on Gull Rocks to help its ships travel safely up and down Narragansett Bay. John Swan, an employee of the company, would row out to the rocks and sit under a shelter, blowing a horn as a warning to oncoming steamers.

Gull Rocks Lighthouse was automated in 1960. In 1961 the Coast Guard burned down the lighthouse.

Courtesy of Coast Guard Historian's Office

A skeleton tower was built at Gull Rocks Lighthouse in 1928.

Courtesy of Coast Guard Historian's Office

Gull Rocks Lighthouse was discontinued in 1969, when the Newport Bridge was finished. The skeleton tower was removed in 1970.

A 375 mm lens was installed on the skeleton tower in 1939.

The fog bell was located next to the skeleton tower.

Gull Rocks today.

3 gallons Oil reservoir

Float Chamber

Lens lanterns like the one above were hung from the east and west gables at Gull Rocks
Lighthouse.

Hog Island Shoal Lights

Hog Island Shoal Lightship: LV-12
1885–1901

Hog Island Shoal Lighthouse
1901–present

Hog Island Shoal Lightship: LV-12

Ship Designation: LV-12

Location: Southeast end of Hog Island Shoal

Year Built: 1846

Design: Wood - white oak and locust; copper and galvanized iron fastenings; 2 masts; lantern and square day mark on foremast only

Length: 72' (lbp) **Beam:** 20' 6" **Draft:** 9' 7" **Tonnage:** 159 gross

Illuminating Apparatus: Single lantern on foremast, 8 oil lamps with reflectors

Propulsion: Sail - schooner rig

Years on Station: 1885–1901

Status: Sold at auction in 1903

Light Characteristic: Occulting White every 4 seconds

Range: 4 miles

Courtesy of Nation al Archives and James Claflin

This is the daymark on the mast of Hog Island Shoal Lightship LV-12.

Hog Island Shoal Lightship LV-12 was placed on Hog Island Shoal in 1886. It replaced a private lightship maintained by the Old Colony Steamboat Company.

Courtesy of National Archives and James Claflin

M.L.S.   -Copy-   2227.

Light-House Establishment,

General Depot,

B 1787   Office of Inspector, 3d District,
Inclosures.

ETO   Tompkinsville,N.Y.,February 12,1903.

Subject: Light-Vessel No.12-
          Report of sale at public auction-

The LIGHT-HOUSE BOARD,

    Washington, D.C.

Sirs:

    Referring to the Board's communication (File No. 2227) of
8th December, 1902, directing that Light-Vessel No. 12,lately
at Hog Island Shoal, R.I., be disposed of at public auction,etc.;

    I have the honor to report that the sale of the vessel above
referred to was consummated at New London, Conn., on 9th February, 1903.

purchaser, at the sum of Three hundred sixty dollars ($360.00).

    My accounts for this sale will be forwarded to the Auditor,
through the Board, as soon as convenient.

                    Respectfully,

                        (Signed) Wm. M. Folger,

                                Captain, U.S.N.,
                                    Inspector.

Letter about the sale of Hog Island Shaol LV 12.

Hog Island Shoal Lighthouse

Location: Entrance to Mount Hope Bay

Established: 1901

Lighthouse Constructed: 1901

Automated: 1964

Original Illuminating Apparatus: Fifth-order Fresnel lens

Current Illuminating Apparatus: 250 mm lens

Height: 60 feet

Status: Active aid to navigation

Light Characteristic: Isophase White every 6 seconds

Range: 12 miles

Hog Island Shoal Lighthouse was built in 1901 to replace Hog Island Shoal Lightship LV-12.

Courtesy of Coast Guard Historian's Office

Hog Island Shoal Lighthouse in 1902.

Courtesy of Coast Guard Historian's Office

Hog Island Shoal Lighthouse's lantern.

Courtesy of Coast Guard Historian's Office

Hog Island Shoal Lighthouse's pier deck.

Courtesy of Coast Guard Historian's Office

A keeper, possibly Adolph Aronson, is standing near the foghorn on Hog
Island Shoal Lighthouse.

In 2004, Hog Island Shoal Lighthouse was offered, through the National Historic Lighthouse Preservation Act, to local governments and preservation groups. In 2006 after no local government or preservation groups showed interest in acquiring the lighthouse, the General Service Administration put the lighthouse up for sale. It was sold in August 2006 for $165,000.

Lime Rock Lighthouse
(Ida Lewis Lighthouse)

Location: Newport Harbor

Established: 1854

Current Lighthouse Constructed: 1854

Deactivated: 1927

Original Illuminating Apparatus: Sixth-order Fresnel lens

Current Illuminating Apparatus: None

Height: 13 feet

Status: Yacht Club

Light Characteristic: None

Range: None

In 1854, a square granite tower was built on Lime Rock in Newport Harbor. It was equipped with a sixth order Fresnel lens. A small one-room building was built on Lime Rock to serve as a temporary shelter if the keeper couldn't get back to shore. In 1856, a permanent keeper's dwelling was attached to the tower.

Ida Lewis was the keeper at Lime Rock Lighthouse from 1879 until her death in 1911.

Frank Leslie's Illustrated Newspaper (November 5, 1881)
Ida Lewis and the medal she was awarded by The Humane Society Of Massachusetts.

Ida Lewis in the backyard of Lime Rock Lighthouse.

Ida Lewis standing behind Lime Rock Lighthouse with two women. The photograph does not identify which of the women is Ida Lewis. I believe the woman in the middle is Ida.

Lime Rock Lighthouse was equipped with a sixth order Fresnel lens.

Lime Rock Lighthouse and Ida Lewis. Her annual salary was $750.00.

A postcard of Newport showing Lime Rock Lighthouse.

Lime Rock Lighthouse and the city of Newport.

In 1925 the Lighthouse Service changed the name of Lime Rock Lighthouse to Ida Lewis Lighthouse to honor Ida. It was closed in 1927 and was sold the following year for $7,200.

Courtesy of Coast Guard Historian's Office

Ida Lewis Lighthouse was deactivated on July 25, 1927 and was replaced with a thirty foot skeleton tower. The tower was removed in 1963.

The skeleton tower and 200 mm lantern at Ida Lewis Lighthouse.

Courtesy of Coast Guard Historian's Office

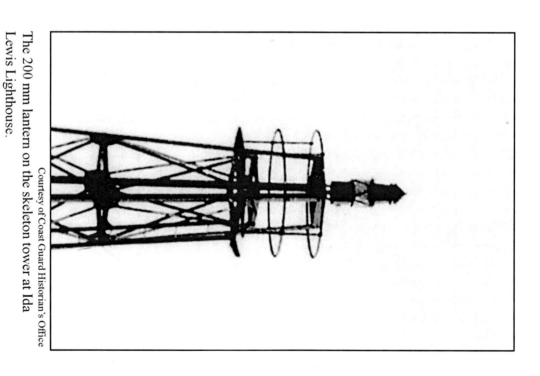

The 200 mm lantern on the skeleton tower at Ida Lewis Lighthouse.

Courtesy of Coast Guard Historian's Office

Frank Leslie's Illustrated Newspaper (November 5, 1881)

Lime Rock Lighthouse at night.

Frank Leslie's Illustrated Newspaper (November 5, 1881)
Ida Lewis lighthing the lamp at Lime Rock Lighthouse.

Frank Leslie's Illustrated Newspaper (November 5, 1881)

A drawing of Ida Lewis rescuing a soldier from Newport Harbor.

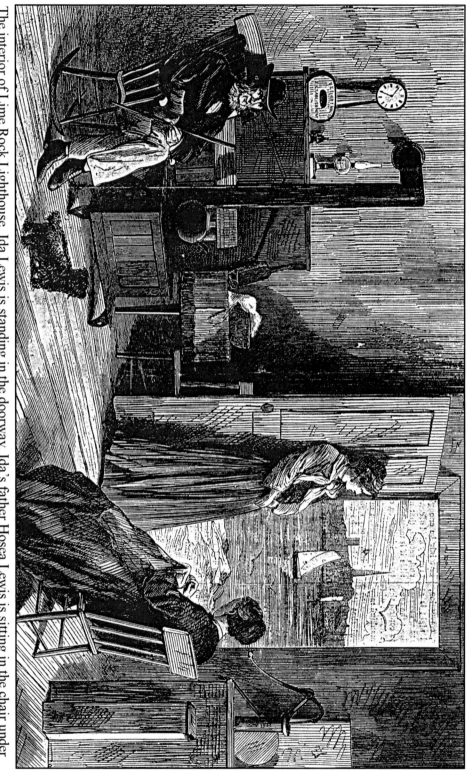

The interior of Lime Rock Lighthouse. Ida Lewis is standing in the doorway. Ida's father Hosea Lewis is sitting in the chair under the clock. Ida's mother Zoraida Lewis is sitting in the chair near the door. The sketch is from the July 31, 1869 edition of *Harper's Weekly.*

The exterior of Lime Rock Lighthouse. Ida Lewis is walking toward the dock. The sketch is from the July 31, 1869 edition of *Harper's Weekly.*

Mussel Bed Shoals Lighthouse

Location: Entrance to Mount Hope Bay

Established: 1873

Lighthouse Constructed: 1873

Removed: 1939

Original Illuminating Apparatus: Six-order Fresnel lens

Current Illuminating Apparatus: 250 mm Lens

Height: 19 feet

Status: Active aid to navigation - Skeleton tower

Light Characteristic: Flashing Red every 6 seconds

Range: 6 miles

Mussel Shoal Light House, NARRAGANSETT BAY, R. I.   10579

Musselbed Shoal Lighthouse's first keeper was Dennis Shea. He was appointed on August 5, 1873.

Courtesy National Archives, photo no. 26-G-8-54

During the winter of 1875, Musselbed Shoal Lighthouse was damaged by an ice floe. It moved the lighthouse's stone foundation four feet. In 1878 the lighthouse was taken ashore and the stone foundation was replaced with a larger granite one. The lighthhouse was put on the granite foundation when it was completed.

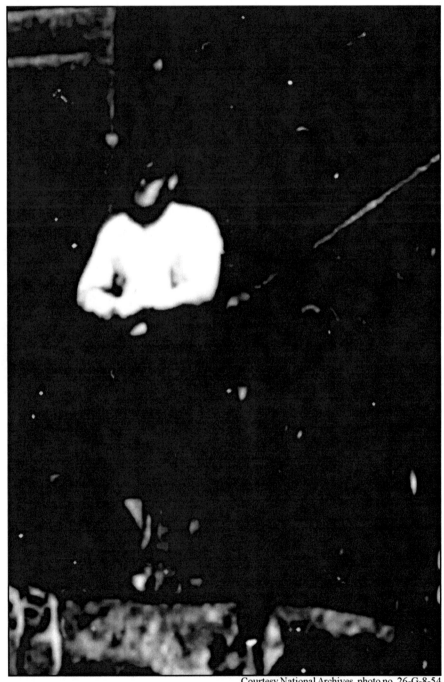

A Musselbed Shoal lighthouse keeper, possibly William Tengren, relaxing.

Musselbed Shoal lighthouse's lantern and sixth order Frensel lens.

Courtesy National Archives, photo no. 26-G-8-54

Musselbed Shoal lighthouse's fogbell. It was rung by a machine at intervals of 20 seconds.

Courtesy of N.L. Stebbins

Musselbed Shoal Lighthouse was badly damaged during the 1938 Hurricane. It was torn down in 1939 and was replaced with a skeleton tower.

Musselbed Shoal Lighthouse's base and skeleton tower.

Nayatt Point Lighthouse

Location: Nayatt Point at the entrance to the Providence River

Established: 1828

Current Lighthouse Constructed: 1856

Deactivated: 1868

Original Illuminating Apparatus: Fifth-order Fresnel lens

Current Illuminating Apparatus: None

Height: 25 feet

Status: Private Residence

Light Characteristic: None

Range: None

Nayatt Point Light and keeper's house.

Nayatt Point Lighthouse was sold at auction at the Custom House in Providence, Rhode Island on August 9, 1890 for $4,000.

Nayatt Point Lighthouse at low tide in the late 1800's. The shoals near the lighthouse are visible.

Nayatt Point Lighthouse as it looks today.

Nayatt Point Light-tower and the attached oil cleaning room in the late 1800s.

Nayatt Point Lighthouse's Keeper's house in the late 1800s.

The first Nayatt Point Lighthouse's tower was built in 1828. It was damaged in an 1855 storm, and replaced with this light tower in 1856.

Nayatt Point Lighthouse's lantern in the late 1800s.

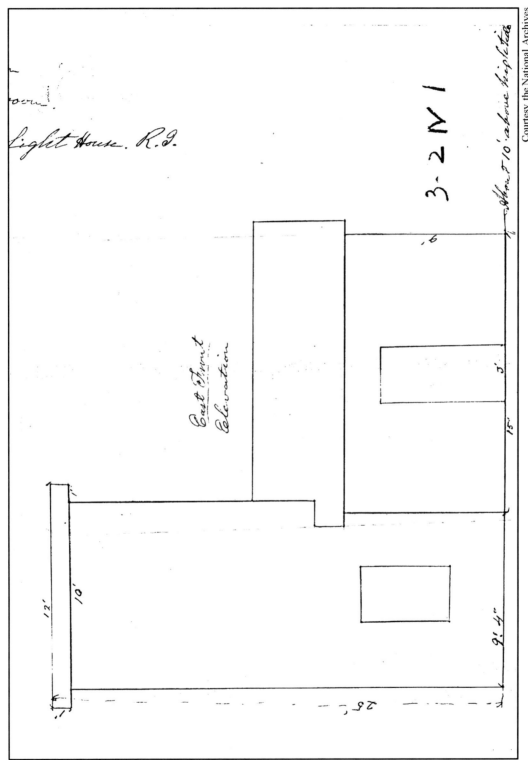

Elevation plans of the second light tower and oil cleaning room built at Nayatt Point. The plans were made on September 9, 1856.

Courtesy the National Archives

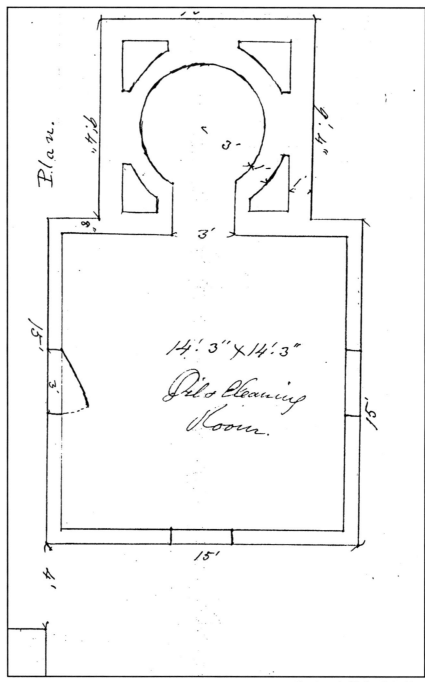

Plan.

14' 3" X 14' 3"
Oil Cleaning
Room.

Interior plans of the second light tower and oil cleaning room built at
Nayatt Point. The plans were made on September 9, 1856.

Newport Harbor Lighthouse
(Goat Island Lighthouse)

Location: North end of Goat Island

Established: 1823

Current Lighthouse Constructed: 1842

Automated: 1923

Original Illuminating Apparatus: Eight lamps with reflectors

Current Illuminating Apparatus: 300 mm lens

Height: 35 feet

Status: Active aid to navigation - Leased to the American Lighthouse Foundation

Light Characteristic: Fixed Green

Range: 11 miles

Courtesy of N.L. Stebbins

The first Goat Island Lighthouse was built in 1823. It was closed in 1842 and was replaced with the lighthouse above.

Courtesy National Archives, photo no. 26-LG-12-1

In 1838 construction started on a breakwater from Goat Island to a stone pier and unfinished granite light tower. The breakwater was completed in 1842 and the light was moved from the old lighthouse to the new lighthouse. The keeper's dwelling was added the lighthouse in 1864.

Breakwater Light, Entrance to Newport Harbor, Newport, R. I.

Goat Island Lighthouse and fogbell. The small wooden building to the left of the lighthouse contained the fogbell and striking machine.

Goat Island Lighthouse's lantern and fouth order Fresnel lens.

Courtesy National Archives, photo no. 26-LG-12-1

Courtesy of Coast Guard Historian's Office

In 1921 the submarine N-4 hit the breakwater near Newport Harbor Lighthouse and damaged the keeper's dwelling. It was torn down the following year.

In the 1970s the water between Goat Island and the lighthouse was filled in to built a hotel.

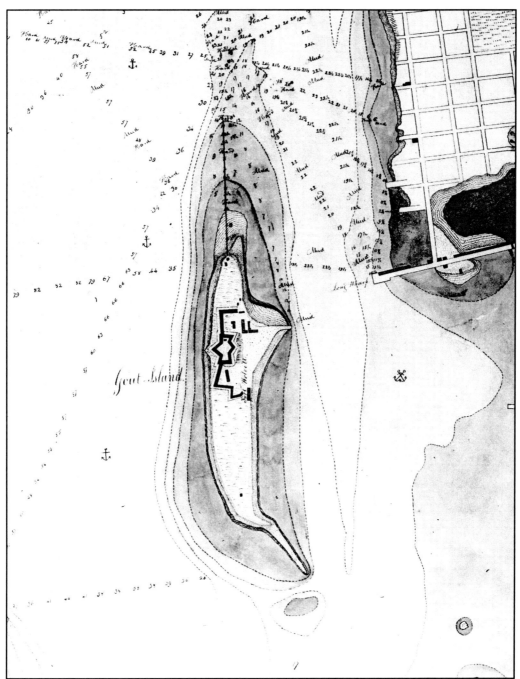

A map of Goat Island in the 1840s.

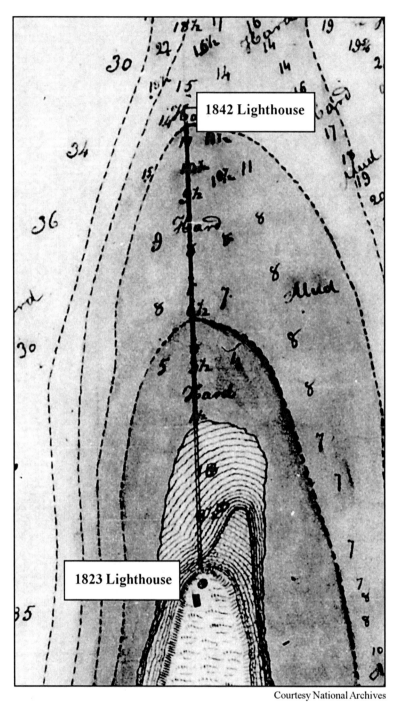

A map of the breakwater at the northern tip of Goat Island in the 1840s. It shows the locations of the 1823 and 1842 Goat Island Lighthouses.

Plum Beach Lighthouse

Location: West Passage of Narragansett Bay near the Jamestown Bridge

Established: 1897

Current Lighthouse Constructed: 1897 - 1899

Deactivated: 1941 - 2003

Reactivated: 2003

Original Illuminating Apparatus: Fourth-order Fresnel lens

Current Illuminating Apparatus: None

Height: 53 feet

Status: Private aid to navigation

Light Characteristic: Flashing White every 5 seconds

Range: 4 to 6 miles

Courtesy of N.L. Stebbins

Construction started on Plum Beach Lighthouse on September 12, 1898, when the partly constructed foundation was lowered onto its present location.

Plum Beach Light, West Passage, Narragansett Bay, R. I.

During construction of Plum Beach Lighthouse's foundation a layer of quicksand was discovered under it. There was not enough money in the budget to fix this problem and complete the lighthouse. Construction was stopped in 1897. The foundation top was covered and a temporary red lantern was placed on it on February 1, 1897.

Courtesy National Archives, photo no. 26-LG-14-9

In 1898 an additional appropriation of $9,000 was approved to finish Plum Beach Lighthouse. It was finally completed on May 30, 1899. Plum Beach Lighthouse's first keeper, Joseph L. Eaton, was appointed on June 5, 1897. He only served for a month at the completed lighthouse before a new keeper replaced him.

After the first Jamestown Bridge was completed in 1941, Plum Beach Lighthouse was closed. By the 1980s, vandals and the weather left the lighthouse in bad shape. In 1988 the Friends of Plum Beach Lighthouse was formed to protect and restore the lighthouse.

In 2003 the Friends of Plum Beach Lighthouse, with a $500,000 federal grant, restored the Plum Beach Lighthouse.

Plum Beach Lighthouse's lantern in the early Twentieth Century. The fourth order Fresnel lens can be seen the lantern.

Plum Beach Lighthouse's unrestored lantern in 1997.

Plum Beach Lighthouse's restored lantern in 2005. A solar powered beacon was placed in the latern in December 2003 and was relit as a private aid to navigation. The beacon and a set of solar panels can be seen in the lantern.

Courtesy National Archives, photo no. 26-LG-14-9

Plum Beach Lighthouse's pier deck in the early Twentieth Century.

Plum Beach Lighthouse's unrestored pier deck and foundation in 1997. The stones around the foundation were added in 1922.

Plum Beach Lighthouse's restored pier deck and foundation in 2005.

Point Judith Lighthouse

Location: Point Judith

Established: 1810

Current Lighthouse Constructed: 1857

Automated: 1954

Original Illuminating Apparatus: Ten lamps with 15 inch reflectors

Current Illuminating Apparatus: Fourth-order Fresnel lens

Height: 51 feet

Status: Active aid to navigation

Light Characteristic: Group Occulting White every 15 seconds

Range: 16 miles

Courtesy of N.L. Stebbins

The first Point Judith light was a wooden structure built in 1810. It was destroyed during a hurricane in 1815. The current Point Judith Lighthouse was built in 1857.

In 1872 a life saving station, the two buildings on the left side of this postcard, was built near Point Judith Lighthouse.

In 1899 the color of the tower was changed from all white to the upper half being brown and the lower half being white.

In January 1907, a new fourth order Fresnel lens and vapor lamp were installed at Point Judith Lighthouse.

This keeper's dwelling was built in 1856. It replaced an earlier seven room wooden keeper's dwelling.

Point Judith Lighthouse's fog signal, tower, and keeper's dwelling in the late 1800s.

Courtesy National Archives, photo no. 26-LG-14-17

Courtesy National Archives, photo no. 26-LG-14-17

The two men sitting in front of Point Judith Lighthouse keeper's dwelling could be the keeper Joseph Whaley and his son Henry A. Whaley, an assistant keeper. Henry was appointed keeper in 1889, when his father retired.

Courtesy National Archives, photo no. 26-LG-14-17

Point Judith Lighthouse's first steam powered fog signal, a trumpet operated by a Wilcox hot air engine, was installed in 1867. It was replaced with a first class siren in 1872. The siren was amplified by the horn on the outside of the building.

Point Judith Lighthouse and fog signal building in the early 1900s.

In 1902 the steam power plant at the Point Judith Lighthouse's fog signal was replaced by two 16 horsepower engines.

Courtesy National Archives, photo no. 26-LG-14-17

Point Judith Lighthouse's lantern in the 1890s.

Point Judith Lighthouse's lantern in 2001.

Point Juidith Lighthouse in 1932.

A keeper can be seen in Point Judith Lighthouse's lantern, inspecting the Fresnel lens.

The connector between Point Judith Lighthouse and its keeper's dwelling.

Courtesy of Coast Guard Historisn's Office

Point Judith Lighthouse and Coast Guard Station in the early 1940s.

Courtesy of Coast Guard Historisn's Office

Point Judith Lighthouse and keeper's dwelling in the early 1940s. The keeper's dwelling was torn down in 1954.

Point Judith Lighthouse after the keeper's dwelling was removed. The lighthouse's fourth order Fresnel lens can be seen in the lantern.

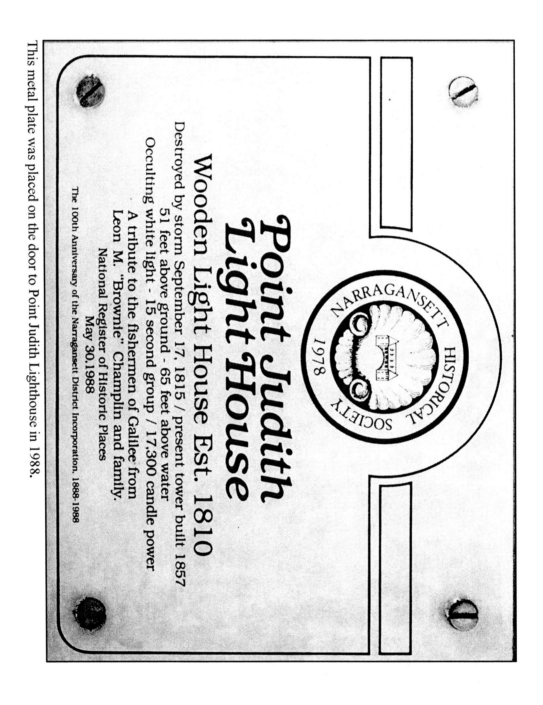

Point Judith
Light House

Wooden Light House Est. 1810

Destroyed by storm September 17, 1815 / present tower built 1857
51 feet above ground - 65 feet above water
Occulting white light - 15 second group / 17,300 candle power

A tribute to the fishermen of Galilee from
Leon M. "Brownie" Champlin and family,
National Register of Historic Places
May 30,1988

The 100th Anniversary of the Narragansett District Incorporation, 1888-1988

This metal plate was placed on the door to Point Judith Lighthouse in 1988.

Pomham Rocks Lighthouse

Location: East side of Providence River

Established: 1871

Current Lighthouse Constructed: 1871

Deactivated: 1974–2006

Original Illuminating Apparatus: Six-order Frensel lens

Current Illuminating Apparatus: 250 mm lens

Height: 40 feet

Status: Private aid to naviagtion - Owned by Mobil Oil Company

Light Characteristic: Fixed Red

Range: 6 miles

C.H. Salisbury was appointed Pomham Rocks Lighthouse's first keeper on December 4, 1871 and remained at the lighthouse until his death in 1893. His wife, Mary A. Salisbury, replaced him, but only served as the keeper for a few months.

Pomham Rocks Lighthouse was closed in 1974 and was replaced with a skeleton tower.

In July 1980, the General Service Administration, the government agency responsible for disposing of unneeded government property, put Pomham Rocks Lighthouse up for auction. It received thirty bids for the light. On August 12, the bids were opened. The high bid, $40,100, was placed by the Mobil Oil Corporation (now Exxon Mobil), who has a terminal nearby.

In 2005, Exxon Mobil leased the Pomham Rocks Lighthouse to the American Lighthouse Foundation. On a June 6, 2005 ceremony at Pomham Rocks Lighthouse, the Friends of Pomham Rocks Lighthouse and the American Lighthouse Foundation awarded a $300,000 contract to Abcore Restoration to repair and restore the lighthouse. In 2006, after the exterior restoration was completed, the Coast Guard to moved the light back to the lighthouse. On August 30, 2006 the light was officially relighted by Rhode Island Governor Donald Carcieri.

Poplar Point Lighthouse

Location: Entrance to Wickford Harbor

Established: 1831

Lighthouse Constructed: 1831

Discontinued: 1882

Original Illuminating Apparatus: Eight Argand Lamps with reflectors

Current Illuminating Apparatus: None

Height: 37 feet

Status: Private Residence

Light Characteristic: None

Range: None

Poplar Point Lighthouse in 2000.

Wickford, R.I., Old Light House.

From Mother.

Poplar Point Lighthouse was built by Charles Allen in 1831. He was paid $1,889 to build it.

Poplar Point Lighthouse as it looked in 1882.

Poplar Point Lighthouse was closed in 1882. It was sold at a public auction on October 1894. The high bidder, Albert Sherman, paid $3,944.67 for it.

Poplar Point Lighthouse in the early twentieth century.

Wickford Harbor, R.I. – Keeper – Transfer to, requested

Treasury Department,

OFFICE OF THE LIGHT-HOUSE BOARD,

Washington, Oct. 10th 1882

Sir:

A new light-house and fog-signal having been erected on Old Gay Rock, Wickford Harbor, R.I., and known as the Wickford Harbor Light, to replace the one at Poplar Point, the Board has the honor to request the transfer of Mr. Henry F. Sherman, Keeper at the latter place to be Keeper of the new station, from November 1, 1882, on which date it will be lighted; Mr. Sherman to receive the same salary of $480 per annum.

It is also requested that like Poplar Point the station be

Courtesy of the National Archives

The first page of an October 10, 1882 letter to the Office of the Lighthouse Board requesting the transfer of Poplar Point Lighthouse's keeper Herny Sherman to Wickford Harbor Lighthouse.

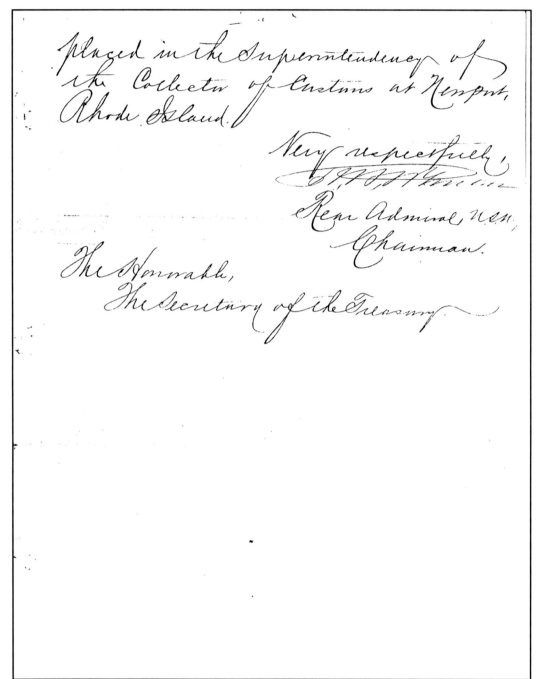

The second page of an October 10, 1882 letter to the Office of the Lighthouse Board requesting the transfer of Poplar Point Lighthouse's keeper Herny Sherman to Wickford Harbor Lighthouse.

Prudence Island Lighthouse

Location: Sandy Point on the east side of Prudence Island

Established: 1852

Current Lighthouse Constructed: 1923

Automated: 1939

Original Illuminating Apparatus: Fifth-order Fresnel lens

Current Illuminating Apparatus: 250 mm lens

Height: 30 feet

Status: Active Aid to Navigation

Light Characteristic: Flashing Green every 6 seconds

Range: 6 miles

Prudence Island Lighthouse was built on Goat Island in 1823. It was moved to Prudence Island in 1852.

Courtesy of Coast Guard Historisn's Office

The wooden structure next to the light was a fogbell and its striking machine. It worked like a clock. The keeper would wind it up and it would strike the bell until it ran down. Its striking machine was either a Stevens or a number 4 Gamewell.

In 1869, the keeper's house was badly damaged during the September 8th hurricane.

Courtesy of N.L. Stebbins

During the Hurricane of 1938, a former Prudence Island Lighthouse keeper, Martin Thompson, along with James Lynch and his wife Ellen, sought refuge with the light's keeper, George Gustavus, and his family in the keeper's dwelling. A tidal surge swept up Narragansett Bay, destroying the keeper's dwelling. The people inside were all swept into the bay. Only the keeper survived. He was pulled to safety by 18 year old George Taber. The surge also damaged the light.

Rose Island Lighthouse

Location: Newport Harbor

Established: 1870

Lighthouse Constructed: 1870

Deactivated: 1971–1993

Original Illuminating Apparatus: Sixth-order Fresnel lens

Current Illuminating Apparatus: PLAT-120-69W-STD-PE-DH Navigation Light

Height: 35 feet

Status: Private aid to navigation

Light Characteristic: Flashing White every six seconds

Range: 6 miles

Rose Island Light, Newport, R. I.

Rose Island Lighthouse's first keeper, John Bailey Cozzeus, was appointed on November 25, 1869. He served to 1872. His annual salary was $500.00.

Courtesy of N.L. Stebbins

A fog bell tower was built at Rose Island in 1885. It's the wooden structure on left side of the lighthouse.

Rose Island Lighthouse was closed in 1971. After years of neglect and vandalism, the Rose Island Lighthouse Foundation restored the lighthouse and relit it as a private aid to navigation in 1993.

Sabin Point Lighthouse

Location: Providence River near Sabin Point

Established: 1872

Lighthouse Constructed: 1872

Burned: 1968

Original Illuminating Apparatus: Six-order Fresnel lens

Current Illuminating Apparatus: None

Height: 36 feet

Status: Burned down in 1968

Light Characteristic: None

Range: None

Sabin Point Lighthouse's first lighthouse keeper was Joseph Bowes. He served from 1872 to 1875.

Courtesy National Archives, photo no. 26-LG-9-58

Sabin Point Lighthouse cost $42,000 to build..

Sabin Point Lighthouse's lantern.

Courtesy National Archives, photo no. 26-LG-9-58

A 160 pound fogbell and a 10,000 blow striking machine was installed at Sabin Point in 1900. It would strike the bell every nine seconds.

Courtesy National Archives, photo no. 26-LG-9-58

A lighthouse keeper's wife and child.

Sabin's Point Light House, NARRAGANSETT BAY, R. I.   10583

On July 3, 1968 Sabin Point Lighthouse was burned by order of the Rhode Island Division of Harbors and Rivers. They wanted to widen and deepen the Providence River but the lighthouse was in the way.

Sabin Point Lighthouse was replaced by a light on a group of pilings called a dolphin. The new Sabin Point Light was later renamed Sabin Point Light 32A. It was discontinued in 1989 and was renamed Sabin Point Daybeacon SP.

Sakonnet Point Lighthouse

Location: On Little Cormorant Rock at the entrance to the Sakonnet River

Established: 1884

Lighthouse Constructed: 1884

Deactivated: 1955 - 1997

Original Illuminating Apparatus: Fourth-order Frensel lens

Current Illuminating Apparatus: 300 mm lens

Height: 66 feet

Status: Active aid to navigation - Owned by Friends of Sakonet Lighthouse

Light Characteristic: Flashing White every 6 seconds

Range: 7 miles

Courtesy of N.L. Stebbins

Sakonnet Point Light in 1898.

Sakonnet Point Lighthouse in the early 1900s.

SAKONNET LIGHTHOUSE, SAKONNET, R. I.

Sakonnet Point Lighthouse was closed from 1955 to 1997.

Courtesy of Coast Guard Historisn's Office

Sakonnet Point Lighthouse in 1944.

Courtesy of Coast Guard Historian's Office

Sakonnet Point Lighthouse's lantern and Fourth Order Frensel Lens .

Courtesy of Coast Guard Historian's Office

Sakonnet Point Lighhouse's foundation and enclosed pier deck.

Sakonnet Point Lighthouse's pier deck and landing platform.

Sakonnet Point Lighthouse's enclosed pier deck and landing platform.

Sakonnet Point Lighthouse's boats and landing platform.

Sakonnet Point Lighthouse today. The enclosed pier deck and landing platform has been removed.

Sassafras Point Lighthouse

Location: Off Sassafras Point in the Providence River

Established: 1872

Lighthouse Constructed: 1872

Removed: 1912

Original Illuminating Apparatus: Six-order Fresnel lens

Current Illuminating Apparatus: None

Height: 14 feet

Status: No Longer Exists

Light Characteristic: None

Range: None

John J. Mullen was Sassafrass Point Light's last keeper. He served fron 1887 until it was discontinued in 1912.

Sassafras Point Light was removed in 1912, when the channel was widened.

A distance view of Sassafras Point Light. It can be seen in the center of the postcard.

Warwick Lighthouse

Location: Warwick Neck

Established: 1826

Current Lighthouse Constructed: 1932

Automated: 1985

Original Illuminating Apparatus: Eight Lamps with reflectors

Current Illuminating Apparatus: 250 mm lens

Height: 39 feet

Status: Active aid to navigation

Light Characteristic: Single Occulting Green every 4 seconds.

Range: 12 miles

Courtesy of N.L. Stebbins

The first Warwick Lighthouse is the building in the middle of photograph. It was built in 1826. The wooden structure on the left side of the lighthouse is the fog signal.

In 1856, a fifth order Fresnel lens, made by Henry Lepait of Paris, was installed at Warwick Lighthouse.

The Warwick Lighthouse served as the keeper's dwelling until 1889, when a seprate one was built. The building on the right was the new keeper's dwelling.

Courtesy of Coast Guard Historian's Office

A blower siren fog signal was installed in the Warwick Lighthouse in 1900. It sounded a continuous blast during foggy weather. The horn can seen on the left side of the lighthouse.

The current Warwick Lighthouse was built in 1932. The 1938 Hurricane eroded the cliff near the lighthouse, leaving it inches from Narragansett Bay. It had to be moved or it would slide into Narragansett Bay. In 1939, the light was moved to its present location. It had to be placed on an eight-foot concrete base because the roof of the keeper's dwelling blocked some ships from seeing it. The light was automated in 1986, when the fourth order Fresnel lens was replaced with a 250mm lens. The keeper's dwelling is still used by the Coast Guard as living quarters for it personnel.

Watch Hill Lighthouse

Location: Watch Hill

Established: 1807

Current Lighthouse Constructed: 1856

Automated: 1986

Original Illuminating Apparatus: Fourth-order Frensel lens

Current Illuminating Apparatus: FRB-300 mm

Height: 45 feet

Status: Active Aid to Navigation - Museum

Light Characteristic: Alternating White and Red every 5 seconds

Range: 16 miles

The first Watch Hill Lighthouse was built in 1808. The light tower and keeper's dwelling were both built of wood. A new granite tower and brick keeper's dwelling were built in 1856.

Watch Hill Point. Watch Hill, R. I.

Watch Hill Point in 1901.

Watch Hill Lighthouse and lifesaving station. The lighthouse is the large white building on the left. The lifesaving station is the large building on the right. The lifesaving station was closed in 1947.

There were two woman keepers at Watch Hill Lighthouse. Sally Ann Crandall served as a keeper from 1879 to 1888. She was replaced by Fanny K. Schuyler, who served from 1888 to 1891.

The small building behind Watch Hill Lighthouse is the oil house.

The granite seawall at Watch Hill Lighthouse. It was built in 1857 to replace two older seawalls that were being undermined by wave action.

In 1855 Watch Hill Lighthouse keeper 's dwelling was described as having a sitting room, dining room, kitchen, three chambers, a closet-room and house-cellar.

In 1806 the government purchased four arces of lands from George and Thankful Foster on Watch Hill Point to build Watch Hill Lighthouse.

Courtesy National Archives, photo no. 26-LG-14-17

A Watch Hill Lighthouse keeper standing near the lighthouse. The identity of keeper is uncertain. It could be Joseph T. Fowler or Julius B. Young.

Courtesy National Archives, photo no. 26-LG-14-17

Watch Hill Lighthouse's original Frensel lens was removed in 1898 and was replaced with a fourth order Frensel lens.

Watch Hill Lighthouse was automated in 1986. It was leased to the Watch Hill Lightkeepers Association. They maintain the lighthouse and run a small museum that contains the lighthouse's Frensel lens.

Watch Hill Lighthouse's lantern in 2000. A VBR-25 rotating beacon can be seen in the lantern.

6.E.

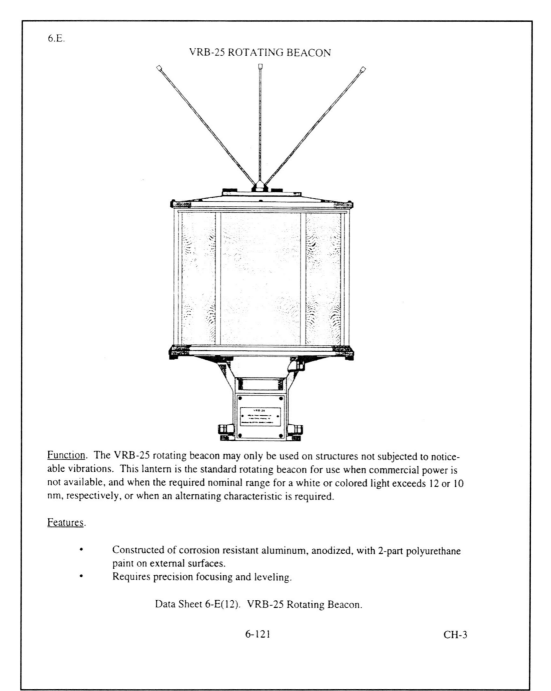

VRB-25 ROTATING BEACON

Function. The VRB-25 rotating beacon may only be used on structures not subjected to notice-able vibrations. This lantern is the standard rotating beacon for use when commercial power is not available, and when the required nominal range for a white or colored light exceeds 12 or 10 nm, respectively, or when an alternating characteristic is required.

Features.

- Constructed of corrosion resistant aluminum, anodized, with 2-part polyurethane paint on external surfaces.
- Requires precision focusing and leveling.

Data Sheet 6-E(12). VRB-25 Rotating Beacon.

6-121   CH-3

The first page of a data sheet for the VBR-25 rotating beacon.

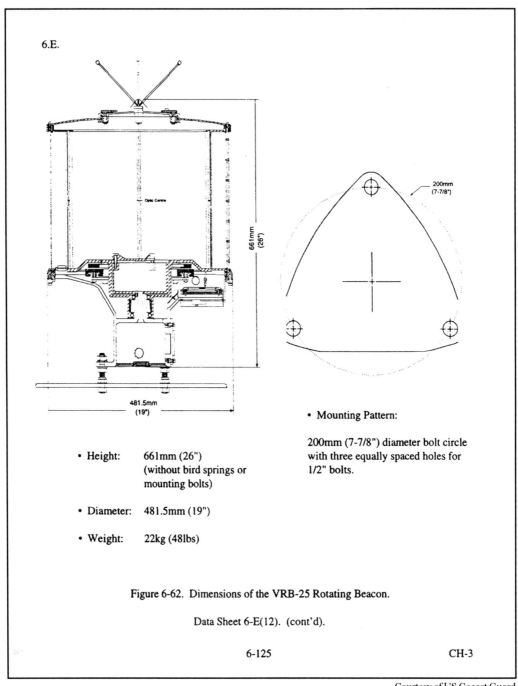

6.E.

661mm (26")

481.5mm (19")

200mm (7-7/8")

• Mounting Pattern:

200mm (7-7/8") diameter bolt circle
with three equally spaced holes for
1/2" bolts.

• Height: 661mm (26")
              (without bird springs or
              mounting bolts)

• Diameter: 481.5mm (19")

• Weight: 22kg (48lbs)

Figure 6-62. Dimensions of the VRB-25 Rotating Beacon.

Data Sheet 6-E(12). (cont'd).

6-125   CH-3

The second page of a data sheet for the VBR-25 rotating beacon.

Whale Rock Lighthouse

Location: Entrance to West Passage of Narragansett Bay

Established: 1882

Lighthouse Constructed: 1882

Destroyed: 1938

Original Illuminating Apparatus: Fourth-order Fresnel lens

Current Illuminating Apparatus: None

Height: 73 feet

Status: Destroyed during the 1938 Hurricane

Light Characteristic: None

Range: None

The Whale Rock Light, Narragansett Pier, R. I.

Whale Rock Lighthouse was first lighted on October 15, 1882.

Courtesy of National Archives
Whale Rock Lighthouse before it was destroyed during the 1938 Hurricane.

Courtesy of National Archives

Whale Rock Lighthouse's lantern and watchroom.

Courtesy of National Archives

Whale Rock Lighthouse's pier deck and landing platform.

Whale Rock Lighthouse after the 1938 Hurricane. Whale Rock Lighted Whistle
Buoy 3 was placed near it as a replacement for the lighthouse. It was later
changed to a gong after people complained about the mournful depressing sound
made by the buoy's whistle

A skeleton tower was placed on Whale Rock Lighthouse's base in 1939.

Courtesy of Coast Guard Historian's Office

It cost $6,200 to repair Whale Rock Lighthouse's base and build the skeleton tower on it.

Courtesy of Coast Guard Historian's Office

The skeleton tower on the base of Whale Rock Lighthouse was equipped with a 375 mm lantern with an acetylene flasher. Acetylene gas, stored in eight tanks at the base of the tower, powered the acetylene flasher.

Wickford Harbor Lighthouse

Location: On Old Gay Rock at the entrance to Wickford Harbor

Established: 1882

Lighthouse Constructed: 1882

Removed: 1930

Original Illuminating Apparatus: Fifth-order Fresnel lens

Current Illuminating Apparatus: 250 mm lens

Height: 42 feet

Status: Active aid to navigation - Skeleton tower

Light Characteristic: Flashing Green every 6 seconds

Range: 6 miles

WICKFORD LIGHT. WICKFORD, R. I

Wickford Harbor Lighthouse was built on Old Gay Rock at the entrance to Wickford Harbor.

Courtesy of Coast Guard Historian's Office

Wickford Harbor Lighthouse's first keeper was Henry F. Sherman. He served from 1882 to 1885.

Courtesy of Coast Guard Historian's Office

Wickford Harbor Lighthouse lantern.

Courtesy of Coast Guard Historian's Office

A Wickford Harbor lighthouse keeper.

Wickford Harbor Lighthouse was closed in 1930. It was torn down and replaced with a skeleton tower. By the 1990s the lighthouse's foundation metal frame had badly deteriorated. Sections of the it had fallen away exposing the lighthouse's concrete and brick foundation. It was becoming unstable and needed to be replaced. The foundation was removed and was replaced with a pile of stones. The skeleton tower was put on the pile of stones. The building in the background is Poplar Point Lighthouse.

GLOSSARY

A

Alternating Light - A light showing different colors alternately.

Argand Lamps - They are fountain lamps, consisting of an oil reservoir, a burner with cylindrical wick and lamp chimney, and a reflector.

C

Composite group-flashing light - A group-flashing light in which the flashes are combined in successive groups of different numbers of flashes.

Composite group-occulting light - A light similar to a group-occulting light except that the successive groups in a period have different numbers of eclipses.

E

Eclipse - An interval of darkness between appearances of a light.

F

Fifth-order Fresnel lens - It has a height of 20.1 inches and the focal distance of the lens (the distance from the center of the light to the inner surface of the lens) is 7.4 inches.

First-order Fresnel lens - It has a height of 92.5 inches and the focal distance of the lens (the distance from the center of the light to the inner surface of the lens) is 36.2 inches.

Fixed and Flashing light - A light in which a fixed light is combined with a flashing light of higher luminous intensity.

Fixed and Group Flashing light - A light in which a fixed light is combined with a flashing light of higher luminous intensity, in which a group of flashes, specified in number, is regularly repeated.

Fixed light - A light showing continuously and steadily, as opposed to rhythmic light.

Flashing light - A light in which the total duration of light in each period is clearly shorter than the total duration of darkness and in which the flashes of light are all of equal duration.

Fresnel Lenses: Generally consisting of glass refracting and reflecting prisms mounted in metal frameworks, whose function it is to send rays from the light source in the direction required.

G

Group-flashing light - A flashing light in which a group of flashes, specified in number, is regularly repeated.

Group-occulting light -An occulting light in which a group of eclipses, specified in numbers, is regularly repeated.

I

Interrupted quick light - A quick flashing light in which the rapid alternations are inter-rupted at regular intervals by eclipses of long duration.

Isophase light - A rhythmic light in which all durations of light and darkness are equal.

L

Lantern - A structure that protects the lens and other parts of the lighting apparatus from the weather.

LBP (Length Between Perpendiculars) - The measurement of a ship from the bow waterline to the aft edge of the rudder post.

LOA (Length Overall) - The measurement of a ship from the extreme forward end of the bow to the extreme aft end of the stern.

O

Occulting light - A light in which the total duration of light in each period is clearly longer than the total duration of darkness (eclipses) and in which the intervals of darkness are all equal duration.

Order - The rating used to classify the sizes of Frensel lenses. The order of a lens is classified, by the focal distance of the lens - that is, the distance from the center of the light to the inner surface of the lens.

Q

Quick light - A light in which flashes are produced at a rate of 60 flashes per minute.

S

Second-order Fresnel lens - It has a height of 71.6 inches and the focal distance of the lens (the distance from the center of the light to the inner surface of the lens) is 27.6 inches.

Single-flashing light - A flashing light in which a flash is regularly repeated (frequency not exceeding 30 flashes per minute).

Single Occulting light - An occulting light in which an eclipse is regular repeated.

Sixth-order Fresnel lens - It has a height of 16.1 inches and the focal distance of the lens (the distance from the center of the light to the inner surface of the lens) is 5.9 inches.

Skeleton tower - A tower, usually of steel, constructed of heavy corner members and various horizontal and diagonal bracing members.

T

Third and half-order Fresnel lens - It has a height of 43.3 inches and the focal distance of the lens (the distance from the center of the light to the inner surface of the lens) is 14.7 inches.

Third-order Fresnel lens - It has a height of 55.1 inches and the focal distance of the lens (the distance from the center of the light to the inner surface of the lens) is 19.7 inches.

W

Whistle - A wave actuated sound signal on buoys, which produces sound by emitting compressed air through a circumferential slot into a cylindrical bell chamber.

Bibliography

Abbott, Elizabeth. "A brighter future for Point Judith Light." Providence Journal 15 Apr. 2000: A1+.

Allen, Everett S. *A Wind to Shake the World: The Story of the 1938 Hurricane.* Boston: Little. Brown and Company, 1976.

Bachand, Robert G. *Northeast Lights: Lighthouse and Lightships, Rhode Island to Cape May, New Jersey.* Norwalk: Sea Sports Publications, 1989.

"Block Island South East Lighthouse: National Historic Landmark Study." Reynolds, Andrea E. National Park Service. 8 Sept. 2004 <http://www.cr.nps.gov/maritime/nhl/blockisl.htm>

Bradner, Lawrence H. *Plum Beach Light: The Birth, Life, Death of a Lighthouse.* Wickford: Dutch Island Press, 1989.

"Brenton Lightship Ups Anchor: Tower Take Over." *Providence Journal* 28 Sept. 1962. Evening Bulletin ed.: 24.

Cassinelli, Ron "Enough money in to move lighthouse" *Providence Journal.* 24 Oct. 1991: A3.

Champlin, Richard L. "Rhode Island First Lighthouse." *Newport History* 43 (1970): 49–64.

———. "Rose Island Centennial." *Newport History* 43 (1970): 65–70.

———. "Some Guardians of The East Bay." *Newport History* 43 (1971): 29–62.

Claflin, James. *Lighthouses and Life Saving Along The Connecticut and Rhode Island Coast.* Charleston: Arcadia Publishing, 2001.

Davis, Paul. "Orphan of the West Passage." Providence Journal 22 Nov 1996. South County ed.: C1+.

"Day Are Numbered for Warwick Light; Old Tower to Be Razed After 106Years." *Providence Journal* 6 Aug 1932. Evening Bulletin ed.: 2.

Dean, Cory. "103-yr.-old Pomham Rock Light loses out to automation." *Providence Journal* 18 Mar 1974: A1+.

D'Entremont, Jeremy. "Coast Guard and Campbell Construction Group Complete Major Restoration of Point Judith Lighthouse." *Lighthouse Digest* Sept 2000: 26–27.

———. "Whale Rock's Keeper Walter B Eberle, 1898-1938" *Lighthouse Digest* Apr 2001: 12–13.

———. "Bullocks Point Lighthouse: A Lost Light of the Providence River." *Lighthouse Digest* Aug 2001: 12–13.

"Dutch Island Light May Be Extinguished." *Providence Journal* 8 Feb. 1972: 7.

Fleming, Peyton. "Coast Guard awards contract to dismantle Brenton Tower." *Providence Journal* 26 Aug. 1992: D5.

———. "Ruling dims hopes of lighthouse painter." *Providence Journal* 25 Mar 1992. South County ed.: B1+.

"Foundation to recieve title to Block Island lighthouse." *Providence Journal.* 31 May 1991: A8.

"Gasoline-Filled Tanker Still Burning." *Providence Journal* 8 Aug 1958: 1.

Gleason, Sarah C. *Kindly Lights: A History of the Lighthouses of Southern New England.* Boston: Beacon Press, 1991.

"Gull Rock Light Off to Storage." *Providence Journal* 9 Jan. 1970 Morning Journal ed.: 21

Gunther-Rosenberg, Avis. "Bristol lighthouse cottage has postcard-petty views." *Providence Journal* 17 July 1999: East Bay ed.: E4.

Hamilton, Harry. *Lights & Legends: A Historical Guide To Lighthouse Of Long Island Island Sound, Fisher Island Sound and Block Island South.* Stamford: Wescott Cove Publishing Co., 1987.

Hinckley, Anita W. Wickford Memories. Boston: Branden Press, 1972. 83–86.

Harrison, Timothy. "Autographed Photo of Heroine Donated." *Lighthouse Digest* Feb 2000: 26–27.

———. "Coast Guard Restoring Point Judith Light." *Lighthouse Digest* June 2000: 26–27.

"Ida Lewis: The Newport Heroine." *Harper's Weekly* 31 July 1869. 484.

Jagolinzer, Bob. "Saving a Bay Beacon." Providence Journal 16 Nov 1991. South County ed.: C1+.

King, H. D. Letter to Secretary of Commerce. 16 April 1929. National Archives. Washington, D.C.

Krieger, Elliot. "Mobil has top bid in competition to buy Bay lighthouse." *Providence Journal* 13 Aug. 1980: A6.

Lightships And Lightship Stations Of The United States Government. Ed. Joseph Kiebish. United States Coast Guard. 9 Sept 2004 <http://www.uscg.mil/hq/g-cp/history/LightshipIndex.html>.

"Light Housekeeping." *People* 7 July 1997: 63.

"Lighthouse Blast Hurls 5 Into Air" *Providence Journal* 6 February 1923. Morning Journal ed.: 1.

"Lighthouse For Sale." *Lighthouse Digest* Sept. 1997: 29.

Lord, Peter. "Lighthouse begins trek to safety." *Providence Journal.* 14 Aug. 1993: A1.

———. "All moved up the Block Southeast Lighthouse safely relocated." *Providence Journal.* 6 Dec. 1993: A1.

———. "Lighthouse given another outlook." *Providence Journal.* 12 Aug. 1994: C6.

———. "Block Island celebrates relighting of its lighthouse." *Providence Journal.* 28 Aug. 1994: B1.

McAdam, Roger Williams. *The Old Fall River Line.* New York: Stephen Daye Press, 1937.

Minsinger, William Elliott, comp. *The 1938 Hurricane: A Historical and Pictorial Summary.* Randolph Center: Greenhills Books. 1988.

"New Steel Lightship Replaces "Old No. 39" at Brenton's Reef." Providence Journal 28 Mar. 1935. Morning Journal ed.: 9.

Oliynyk, Sandra. "Block Island's North Light is being relit Ceremony Ceremony to kick off major renovation." *Providence Journal* 2 Aug. 1989, South County Ed., Z-01.

Pina, Alisha A.. "Prudence Island Conservancy gains stewardship of lighthouse" *Providence Journal* 8 Aug 2001, East Bay ed.: C1.

"Pomham Lighthouse Family Finds Life Third of Mile from Shore Has Hazards" *Providence Journal* 2 August 1940. Evening Bulletin ed.: 8.

"Rose Island Gets $400,000 From The State." *Lighthouse Digest* Nov 1998: 13.

Rose Island Lighthouse Foundation About Rose Island Page. Rose Island Lighthouse Foundation, Inc. 14 Sept. 2004. <http://www.roseislandlighthouse.org/roseisle.htm>.

"Sakonnet Lighthouse Saved by Citizens." *Fall River Herald News* 11 Jul. 1956: 1.

Smith, Martha. "THE RESCUED LIGHT For more than a century, Block Island's Southeast Light guided those at sea - serving also, for a remarkable few, as home. Itself recently saved from the sea's destruction, the be... " *Providence Journal.* 21 Aug. 1994, sec. Rhode Island Magazine: M6.

"Storm Wrecks Lighthouse, But Keeper Sticks to Post." *Providence Journal* 6 Oct. 1938. Evening Bulletin ed.: 1.

"Tower signals retirement of lighthouse." *Providence Journal.* 13 Nov. 1989: B1.

"Town Wants to Know Owner Will Care for Old Lighthouse." *Providence Journal* 13 Jul 1956: 8.

"Unattended Beacon Will Replace Eberle Lighthouse." *Providence Journal* 8 Dec. 1939. Evening Bulletin ed.: 1.

United States Coast Guard. *United States Coast Guard Aids to Navigation, 1945.* Washington: GPO, 1946.

United States Lighthouse Service. *Annual Reports.* Washington: GPO, 1838-1905.

Yates, J. T. Letter to Commissioner of Lighthouse. 8 April 1929. National Archives. Washington, D.C.

Index

B

Beavertail Lighthouse, 1–7
Block Island North Lighthouse, 8–10
Block Island Southeast Lighthouse, 11–15
Brenton Reef Lights, 16
Brenton Reef Lighthouse: LV-14, 17
Brenton Reef Lighthouse: LV-11, 18–21
Brenton Reef Lighthouse: LV-39, 22–25
Brenton Reef Lighthouse: LV-102/WAL-525, 26–30
Brenton Reef Offshore Ligth station, 31–33
Bristol Ferry Lighthouse, 37–44
Bullock Point Lighthouse, 45–51

C

Castle Hill Lighthouse, 52–55
Conanicut Lighthouse, 56–62
Conimicut Lighthouse, 63–67

D

Dutch Island Lighthouses, 68–72

F

Fuller Lighthouse, 73–74

G

Gould Island Lighthouse, 75–77
Gull Rocks Lighthouse, 78–85

H

Hog Island Shoals Lights, 86

Hog Island Shoals Lightship: LV-12, 87–89
Hog Island Shoals Lighthouse, 90–94

I

Ida Lewis Lighthouse, 95–109

L

Lime Rock Lighthouse, 95–109

M

Musselbed Shoal Lighthouse, 110–115

N

Narragansett Bay Entrance Lighthed Horn Buoy NB, 34–36
Nayatt Point Lighthouse, 116–122
Newport Harbor Lighthouse, 123–130

P

Plum Beach Lighthouse, 131–138
Point Judith Lighthouse, 139–152
Pomham Rocks Lighthouse, 153–155
Poplar Point Lighthouse, 156–159
Prudence Island Lighthouse, 160–163

R

Rose Island Lighthouse, 164–165

S

Sabin Point Lighthouse, 166–170
Sakonnet Point Lighthouse, 171–177
Sassafras Point Lighthouse, 178–179

W

Warwick Lighthouse, 180–183
Watch Hill Lighthouse, 184–192
Whale Rock Lighthouse, 193–197
Wickford Harbor Lighthouse, 197–201

About the Author

Richard Holmes is the creator of the website Rhodeislandlighthousehistory.info.

Breinigsville, PA USA
22 September 2009
224571BV00001B/3/P

9 780615 263229